Preparing Sunday without the Eucharist

Andrew Britz, osb, and Zita Maier, osu

NOVALIS
THE LITURGICAL PRESS
EJ DWYER

Design: Eye-to-Eye Design, Toronto

Layout: Suzanne Latourelle

Illustrations: Eugene Kral

Series Editor: Bernadette Gasslein

© 1996, Novalis, Saint Paul University, Ottawa, Ontario, Canada

Business Office: Business Office: Novalis, 49 Front Street East, 2nd floor, Toronto, Ontario M5E 1B3

Novalis: ISBN 2 89088 805 3

The Liturgical Press: ISBN 0-8146-2479-0
A Liturgical Press Book
Published in the United States of America by The Liturgical Press, Collegeville, Minnesota 56321

EJ Dwyer: ISBN 0-85574-079-5
EJ Dwyer, Locked Bag 71, Alexandria, NSW 2015, Australia

Printed in Canada.

Canadian Cataloguing in Publication Data

Britz, Andrew, 1940-
    Preparing Sunday without the Eucharist

(Preparing for liturgy)
Includes bibliographic references.
ISBN 2-89088-805-3

    1. Public worship—Catholic Church. 2. Catholic Church—Liturgy. I. Maier, Zita, 1936- II. Title. III. Series.

BX2045.L39B75 1997   264'.02   C96-901081-8

Contents

Introduction

The eucharist celebrates God's victory in our lives. Not surprisingly, the Christian community gathers to worship on the Lord's Day, Sunday, the day of the Lord's resurrection. Christians do not see the eucharist simply as a reminder of the resurrection, but rather as its fullest expression in their lives. Something is fundamentally wrong if they do not celebrate eucharist on the Lord's Day. (For more information and reflection on the Lord's Day, see *Preparing the Liturgical Year* in this series.)

Consequently, the first responsibility of the institutional church is to provide viable Christian communities with the opportunity to gather and express themselves fully in the eucharist, in praise and thanksgiving. The purpose of eucharist, first of all, is to give God thanks and praise and, in doing so, to enable us to stand in awe of what God has done for us and to recognize our great dignity in Christ Jesus.

Sunday Gatherings without Eucharist

In promoting Sunday gatherings of Christian communities in which there is no ordained minister, neither the universal church nor the Canadian church offers these celebrations as a long-term, viable alternative to the eucharist. In an address to the Vatican Congregation for Divine Worship (May 22, 1987), Pope John Paul II noted that the absence of a priest, and thus of the eucharist itself, "is not to be accepted with resignation."

"The current situation must be faced, however," he continues, "and the best provisions must be made for the spiritual welfare of the faithful."

The pope then makes an important assumption as to what these "best provisions" will be: "Now one of the essential points of reference for Christians, from which they draw both light and strength, has been since the beginning the Sunday assembly, the gathering of the faithful in one place to celebrate the risen

Lord." He suggests the community "gather together in praise and petition, in listening to the Word of God and, if possible, in the communion of the eucharistic bread consecrated during an earlier Mass."

Three Critical Functions

These gatherings serve three critically important functions, which provide important criteria by which we can judge the appropriateness and effectiveness of Sunday liturgies without a priest.

Maintaining bonds with the whole church

They "maintain from Sunday to Sunday (the community's) bonds with the whole church." They must bind us to the universal church. The readings should always be those that the church is celebrating in its liturgies throughout the world. The prayers should be those designated in the ritual book for the Sunday.

Desiring the eucharist

These celebrations of the word "do not replace the Mass, but must cause one to desire it all the more." Therefore, these liturgies should not attempt to have the feel of a eucharistic celebration. Rather than give the community a sense that it has fully celebrated its faith, the liturgy should cause the gathering "to desire it (the eucharist) all the more."

A proper celebration of these Sunday liturgies should never mollify the community into accepting its lot, but should rather increase its insistence that the institutional church fulfill its first duty of providing the faithful with the opportunity to celebrate eucharist on the Lord's Day. For all the faithful to be able to celebrate eucharist every Sunday, the priorities and structures of the institutional church will have to change.

For example: Bishop Phaedimus of Amasea felt he could not properly serve the people of Neocaesarea, and since, socially, they could not easily become a part of Amasea, he ordained St. Gregory Thaumaturgos (213-70) as bishop of Neocaesarea. Neocaesarea, according to St. Gregory of Nyssa, had at the time *seventeen* Christians in the community.

About a century later, the Council of Sardica (344 AD) attempted to limit bishops to larger communities, but it insisted that these communities had the right to a priest.

Preserving cohesion and vitality

Sunday celebrations of the word provide "a small community of the faithful a means, although imperfect, of preserving in a concrete manner its cohesion and vitality" (John Paul II). This function is critically important as Canada undergoes massive sociological changes.

Celebrating At Home

In recognizing that liturgy provides "cohesion and vitality" to the community, the pope reminds church leaders to respect the secular structures of the believing community. People have a right to worship where they are planted. The economic earth-shakers might well ignore a small town as meaningless. The church knows better. It recognizes that the social setting of a small community is not accidental to its life.

By inviting the community to place its story on the altar of the Lord, the liturgy recognizes the worth and dignity of the communities of Placentia, Newfoundland; L'Épiphanie, Québec; or Gull Lake, Saskatchewan. It follows in the tradition of the bishop of Amasea, who had no second thoughts about sending St. Gregory Thaumaturgos to the seventeen believers of Neocaesarea.

Of course, the decision to close down a rural community or inner-city parish that has fallen upon hard times is always a tough judgment. But the basic principle must be: If the secular community is viable—that is, if Gull Lake, for example, is an integral part of the life of the members of the worshipping community, then the secular community is part and parcel of the church's celebration.

So while the eucharist is the fullest and highest expression of the church's life, the church cannot, for the sake of its very health, ignore the needs of the parish that lacks a priest but certainly still needs to place its whole life on the altar of the Lord.

In Summary

1. There is no true alternative to eucharist. In it, Christians express fully who they are as church.

2. Sunday celebrations of the word must serve three critical functions:

    • they maintain bonds with the whole church;

    • they cause the assembly to desire the eucharist;

    • they preserve the unity of the local church.

3. People have the right to worship in the community they call home.

Discussion Questions

1. What is the heart of any Christian liturgy? Has this been your experience? Why or why not?

2. Each of the three functions of Sunday gatherings without a priest challenges communities to experience certain things in their celebrations. Ponder the following:

   Does your community have a sense of being bonded to the rest of the church, both local and universal? What factors support your answer?

   Is there a difference between desiring to celebrate eucharist and desiring to share in holy communion? How can you help your community distinguish between these two desires?

   How does your Sunday gathering promote the vitality of your local community?

3. What changes in priorities might promote the kinds of change that would enable each parish to celebrate Sunday eucharist?

CHAPTER 1

The Assembly: the Heart of Christian Liturgy

The heart of any Christian liturgy, with or without a priest, is the assembly. Thus much of this booklet deals with the meaning and function of the assembly in Christian worship.

Assembly as Subject of the Act of Worship

Vatican II's *Constitution on the Sacred Liturgy* sought to re-introduce into the mainstream of church life the understanding that the assembly, in Christ, is the celebrant of the liturgy: "The Church earnestly desires that all the faithful be led to that full, conscious and active participation in liturgical celebrations called for by the very nature of the liturgy" (#14).

The Assembly as Sacrament

Whether a priest presides at its celebration or not, the assembly celebrates as the body of Christ, for it is the community of those who, in baptism, have been sealed with the Spirit of Christ.

The *Constitution on the Sacred Liturgy (CSL)* draws on an image of John's gospel (20:34) that Origen, a Father of the Church, has reworked. While John saw blood and water spring forth from the one reigning on the tree, Origen saw "that from the side of Christ as he slept the sleep of death upon the cross, there came forth the wondrous sacrament of the whole church" (*CSL*, #5).

The nature of sacraments

Sacraments are symbols expressing the true nature of our God. Jesus, in his passover from death to newness of life, reveals to us the God we are to celebrate as the meaning of our lives. In breathing forth his Spirit in death, Jesus founded the church, the sacrament of his presence.

This is no static reality. Our ritual actions reveal God's presence. Our sacraments are not water, oil, bread, wine and a sexual relationship, but the community ritualizing its meaning through these common elements. A community breaks bread together, shares a common cup; a Christian couple symbolizes their covenant by their love-making.

We do not receive sacraments: we become them. As the community of faith assembled to celebrate God's unconditional love, we become the sacrament of God.

In liturgy, the community and its ritual action always remain the central focus. In its action with the oil and water, not just in the oil and water themselves, the community celebrates its unity in and with Christ. In anointing, and bathing, in eating and drinking around a common table, this people reveals its deepest meaning.

In communities that cannot have "a complete liturgical celebration of the Lord's Day" (*Directory for Sunday Celebrations in the Absence of a Priest*, #2), the church does not realize the fullness of this sacramental expression. Yet the community is still called to express its sacramentality. Its cohesion and vitality remain the central issues. In experiencing the warmth, the security and the joy of oneness in the community, individuals can go into the world confident of Christ's presence in their life.

The power of the community

St. Augustine, in giving his people an Eastertime instruction dealing with baptism, asks: "Where does the water get so great a power that in touching the body it washes the soul?" (See *On John* 80, 3.) His response is most surprising. He says point blank that it does not come from the word spoken. Rather, Augustine says, the water gets its power "from the word believed," from the community taking hold of the word and transforming it into "a word of faith," to use Augustine's language. The bishop of Hippo goes even further: This word believed is added to the water and it becomes a sacrament, "a visible word."

The ancient church fathers provide another insight. Almost all of them saw the forgiveness of sin as an extension of the mystery of baptism. They saw in the tears of the community for the penitent a revitalization of the waters of baptism. All of them said something like this: Never trust the words of a man (a priest or bishop proclaiming the forgiveness of sin), but rather trust the tears of a mother (the church remembering a child of its own).

St. Jerome says it most bluntly of all. He declares that the keys of binding and loosing belong to the community; thus he can declare quite unequivocally "that the priest cannot restore any one member of the community to spiritual health unless or until all the members of the community together weep with the penitent" (*Dialogue Against the Luciferians*, 5 [PL 23,159]).

Since the 12th century at least we have tended to place the power of the sacraments in the priest, not in the worshipping community. Quite a different dynamic takes over when both priest and people see in the community gathered in worship the power Jesus breathed forth to his church from the cross.

Lay presiders do not have the charism to call forth the church to express its fullness in the eucharist. Yet as they preside over the parish community in any other Sunday liturgy, they are to recognize the living Spirit of God at work, uniting and vivifying the people. Ministering changes subtly—and fundamentally—in those who sees the locus of God's grace in the community, not in themselves as presiders.

A couple of stories illustrate the difference. One afternoon, I walked into a class of Grade 10 students whose interest in school had run its course for the week. Out for a little fun, they decided to give me the silent treatment. Not only would they not talk, but they also made their faces go blank. They completely shut down communication one way. In such a situation, the teacher becomes a babbling idiot in just moments. I knew I had to play their game, find their weakest link and break open a line of communication.

My second story has a liturgical setting. A priest friend was once preaching in an Afro-American parish in Washington, DC. He was not used to members of the congregation speaking up while he was preaching, and so he was a bit startled on hearing one member of the worshipping community shout out, "Alleluia, Father!" It took him a moment or two to recollect his thoughts, and on he went, preaching his Eastertime homily. There were more Alleluias! My friend told me they really ignited him—and he spoke for nearly an hour.

Without the response from faith-filled people, there can be no liturgy. That is Augustine's point: The word gets its power to touch the body and wash the soul, not from the word spoken by the priest, but from its being believed by the people.

Receive Your Own Mystery

St. Augustine, in Sermon 272, teaches: "If you wish to understand the Body of Christ, listen to the Apostle who says to the believers: 'You are the Body of Christ and his members' (1 Cor 12:27). And thus, if you are the Body of Christ and his members, it is your mystery which has been placed on the altar of the Lord; you receive your own mystery. You answer 'Amen' to what you are, and in answering, you accept it. For you hear,

'The Body of Christ,' and you answer, 'Amen.' Be a member of Christ's Body so that your Amen may be true." Although Augustine is speaking about the eucharistic assembly, he highlights some central truths that fit all liturgical celebrations.

Not only is the assembly in Christ the subject of all worship; it also provides the subject matter for worship.

In liturgy, people ritualize their deepest meaning. All Christian liturgies, those with and those without a priest, enable God's people to stand in awe of what God has done with them in making them the body of Christ. Through baptism, Christians are so immersed in Christ that their own story—their own daily dying and rising—mingles with Christ's as the subject matter of their worship.

As the body of Christ, Christians are so implicated in the liturgical action that they celebrate and receive their own deepest meaning around the table of the word and the table of the eucharist. They bring to Sunday liturgy the mystery of their ordinary lives, in their Monday-to-Saturday existence in their communities, large and small, and place them upon the altar of the Lord.

Gathering Up the Community's Faith

The task of each liturgical minister is to gather the faith of the community into a living power that transforms the community. At the eucharist God's Spirit transforms both a people into the body of Christ, and bread and wine into the body and blood of Christ. For both these mighty deeds, God's people stand in awe and give praise and thanksgiving. In its own way this same dynamic is present in every liturgical action.

Proclaiming the Scriptures, Gathering Up Faith

Because Sunday celebrations without eucharist will usually be celebrations of the word, let us look at this dynamic at work in the proclamation of the scriptures.

We have heard again and again that the scriptures are not read in church to teach us. Although liturgy is not didactic, some learning may, of course, happen in a celebration.

Lectors do not proclaim the word to teach the people, but to share God's word that has been filtered through their own faith. To proclaim the scriptures properly, these ministers must have prayed over the word and have struggled with it, so it can express their faith. But if this is the only dynamic at work, it can appear that the lector is foisting his or her faith on the congregation. The community can easily resent that.

Therefore, lectors must also strive to gather up the community's faith and express it in their reading. Eye contact is vital, not so that the lector can get through to the congregation, but so that the community can transform the lector's faith into a communal expression that takes the written word and makes it a living word.

A reflection on God's word is also part of this dynamic. In some places, lay people are mandated to preach; in others, they might present a reflection that has been previously prepared. In either case, it should break open God's word within the life of the community.

As in every liturgy of the word, the intercessions are the community's response in which it prays for the world and for its own needs. The same principles that would apply to the general intercessions at eucharist apply here (*GIRM*, #45-46). This communal expression is especially important for communities that are struggling to stay alive. Smaller rural congregations and inner-city parishes are often subject to fast-moving social influences over which they have little control. In such circumstances it is often difficult for these communities to believe in themselves.

The social difficulties that each community faces provide one more reason for the community to maintain its integrity as a worshipping community. These communities have an added reason for needing someone to be sensitive to their particular problems, someone who can gather up their faith and transform it through the power of the gospel. While liturgies without the charism of presbyteral ministry are never the ideal, there are times and seasons when travelling to the neighbouring parish for a full eucharistic celebration is not what is needed either. If parishioners do this on anything approaching a regular basis, they will quickly undermine the local parish. Soon they will find their parish closed and see the church institution as one more large social entity that has abandoned them.

In Summary

1. The assembly is a sacrament of God, the living symbol of God's presence.

2. The assembly, the body of Christ, is the celebrant of the liturgy and all sacraments. As the body of Christ, the assembly's own story mingles with that of Christ.

3. The task of liturgical ministers is to gather up the community's faith into a living, transforming power.

4. The liturgy of the word is the primary place where this dynamic happens in Sunday celebrations without eucharist.

Discussion Questions

1. What does the term "assembly" mean when we speak of the liturgy?

2. Have you experienced the assembly as doing the liturgy, or do you think and experience that the priest (or presider) is the one who does it? In either case, what led you to experience your role in this manner?

3. Identify how each of the liturgical ministries can fulfill its task as outlined in this chapter. Reflect on your own community's experience. How well are you responding to this task? What would affirm or enhance your abilities?

CHAPTER 2

Communion at Non-eucharistic Celebrations

Sharing in holy communion at full-fledged, non-eucharistic liturgies of the Christian community has not been a normal practice throughout our history. Let us look more closely at this relatively new practice that the church has introduced into its pattern of worship.

Pastoral experience shows the people of God here in Canada clearly wish to share in holy communion at Sunday services, even if no priest is present to celebrate with them in eucharist the fullness of their faith.

Archbishop Francis T. Hurley, who has been bishop in his far-flung diocese of Anchorage, Alaska, since 1976, knows this experience firsthand. The great shortage of priests in his diocese has forced communities to organize Sunday services without a priest. Archbishop Hurley acknowledges that for years he could not convince the people to come out to and express their faith in these celebrations.

All that changed, he notes, when Rome allowed lay people to minister communion at these celebrations. Consequently Archbishop Hurley has become a firm advocate for communion at these lay-led liturgies. He believes his people know the fundamental difference between a full eucharistic celebration and a communion service.

Of course, it is one thing to know the technical difference between a Sunday celebration of the word with communion and the full celebration of the eucharist at which a bishop or priest presides. It is, however, quite another thing for the worshipping community to appreciate the effective difference in their lives.

The eucharistic action—taking, blessing, breaking, and sharing bread—whereby the story of Jesus comes fully alive in the midst of the community and becomes the underpinning of its meaning, cannot be replaced. St. Augustine sees in this identification of Jesus' story with the local church's current story the one acceptable spiritual sacrifice, the meaning of our offering. "Such," he writes, "is the sacrifice of Christians: We, the many, are one body in Christ" (*City of God* 10, 6).

Properly celebrated, Sunday celebrations of the word should lead the community forward, arousing deeper hunger for the fullness of the eucharist. Should a community ever come to see the celebration of Sunday without the eucharist as an effective substitute for Sunday celebration of eucharist, that community is certainly placing itself outside the Catholic experience that has come down to us from the time of the apostles. Since there is a danger of misunderstanding the effective meaning of this communion rite, some theologians (William Marravee's article, "Learning a 'new' eucharistic language "in *Shaping a Priestly People* [Novalis, 1994], is one of the best examples of this position) have asked that it not be practised in Canada. Similarly, some bishops do not allow communion services in their dioceses.

Archbishop Hurley believes that we can make the communion rite at these liturgies a time of hungering for the full expression of the eucharist. So does Pope John Paul II. In his May 22, 1987 speech to the Congregation for Divine Worship, he invites people to forge this connection by partaking, if possible, "in the communion of the eucharistic bread consecrated during an earlier Mass." Allied practices keep this hunger alive. Preparing well, celebrating the communion rite in a low-key manner, and always indicating that communion is connected to the eucharist that is celebrated in another time and place will help. Preaching, too, must foster this hunger, and remind people that the eucharist is our ultimate celebration.

To stress the difference between sharing in holy communion at a lay-led liturgy and doing so at a regular eucharistic celebration, the Canadian bishops, in *Sunday Celebration of the Word and Hours* (Ottawa: CCCB, 1995), ask that the bringing of previously consecrated hosts from the tabernacle be clearly highlighted. The impact of this ritual action will be lost on those parishes where the pastor has ignored the 1967 *Instruction on the Worship of the Eucharist,* which states that the "faithful should receive hosts consecrated at the Mass" (2). Similarly, if during eucharist, both the blessed bread and the cup are shared with people, the absence of the cup will remind participants that this is not a celebration of the eucharist.

A Challenge

As church, we face an immediate challenge: to work single-mindedly so that, in the near future, all of us who are members of the body of Christ can answer the call to come together on the Lord's Day and express fully our praise and joy, our awe and thanksgiving. In the face of this, we must ask—and answer—a crucial question: What shall we do? To avoid misunderstanding, should we limit the eucharistic expression of the people of God who deeply love the eucharist and more than anything else wish to celebrate it in its fullness? Should we insist that the universal institutional church change its priorities on priestly ministry so that we can meet this challenge?

In Summary

1. Sharing in holy communion at non-eucharistic liturgies has not been a normal practice through Christian history.

2. The eucharistic action cannot be replaced.

3. Sunday celebrations of the word should arouse deep hunger for eucharist.

Discussion Questions

1. When you think of eucharistic action, what comes to mind? How can you help your parish community understand the richness of this action?

2. What is the relationship of a communion service to a celebration of the eucharist? What aspects of eucharistic action are missing? What impact does this have on the life of a community?

3. How would you answer the questions in the last paragraph of this chapter? Why?

CHAPTER 3

The Role of the Lay Presider

Leading the church's worship is a ministry done in the name of the community, and since Jesus himself is present whenever the community gathers in his name (Mt 18.20), the ministry of leadership is undertaken in Jesus' name as well. Jesus is the starting point, the first one who prays when the members of his body pray and give thanks. One who presides at prayer in the name of Jesus must first of all believe in him and live as his follower. Only then can a presider authentically gather the prayer of the community in order to offer that prayer with Christ to the Father. This is the essence of all liturgy—prayer. If liturgy is not prayer, it is empty ritualism. Therefore the first question to ask whenever anyone wants to assess whether a community has what might be called "good" liturgy is whether the community prayed when it celebrated the liturgy.

The Presider and the Community

Those called on to lead their communities in Sunday worship need to keep in mind that the liturgy belongs to the community, to the particular community that has gathered for this particular worship and to the whole church. Individuals who are called on to carry out a special ministry in this liturgy do so because the community needs them and calls them. No individual "owns" the liturgy, not even the presider.

At the practical level this means that the presider must have a deep respect for the community that has gathered and a deep respect for the liturgy through which the community worships. A presider sees his or her role as gathering the prayer of the community and shaping it into one prayer, permitting and encouraging the community to speak and to sing with one voice for this is the prayer of the assembly, the body of Christ.

We might ask by whose authority presiders carry out their role. Their ministry serves the community. It means that by their baptism they are called, that they have the gifts to lead the community's prayer, gifts that have been developed through training, and that the community needs their ministry so it can pray in an orderly way. They respond with the leadership needed to empower the community to pray, but this is never a role that allows anyone to overpower others. Presiders are not to dominate, or "lord it over others." All of us are equal before God; the role of leading the community's prayer is never given to reward someone or to satisfy a personal need to serve.

Those called on to be leaders of the assembly's prayer must be alive to the presence of God and attentive to the many ways God is present in all aspects of human life. Seeing the presence of God in their own lives makes it easier for those who lead to see the presence of God in the community. The presider is aflame with God in both life and in liturgy.

A good presider is one who, as a member of the assembly, comes to praise and thank God with the others in the community. The presider prays with the assembly, sings with the assembly, listens with the assembly, keeps silence with the assembly. He or she does all this as one among friends.

The Presider's Skills

Presiders need both organizational skills and flexibility, and the ability to reconcile differences, to communicate reverence for others and for the presence of Christ in the community, to inspire others with their own faith and the faith of those present, and to be concerned for the community.

Presiders must make all feel welcome, unite the community, direct its celebration, enable the other ministries and create reverence towards the presence of God in the community. Leaders do not apologize. ("These poor folks—just because our pastor is away, they have to put up with me again.") Nor do leaders make their way through a liturgy in fear and trepidation lest they make a mistake; being fully prepared is the best antidote to such anxiety. A mistake, which sometimes happens in spite of our best efforts, does not destroy prayer unless we allow it to do so.

Presiders also prepare any comments they add at appropriate times. Leading a community's Sunday worship is a serious responsibility, not a time to "ad lib" or "wing it." Can we expect the spirit of wisdom to do her part if we don't do ours?

Presiders operate, not out of their own needs or likes and dislikes, but in the name of the community, sensitive to its weakness and aware of what goes on there. It is helpful to keep in mind that the church includes weeds as well as wheat. For this reason, ministers need a faith that has matured through inner conversion so they can both foster reconciliation and stand up for what is right, even in their own community. We recognize, too, that we are saved through the church in spite of obvious human frailty.

Discernment

We can ask: Who should be called on to preside when no priest is available for the Sunday eucharist? If a deacon is available, the role would ordinarily fall on him, but most parishes do not have a deacon. The community then, most likely through its parish council, should discern who among them are the leaders who would be accepted by the community and would be most likely to strengthen the community through its prayer. They would look for persons, both women and men, who have gifts of leadership and who are willing to take advantage of any training available, to give time to prepare adequately both in the practical sense and by prayer. No one should be surprised if the most suitable persons to lead the community's prayer are those who also take an active role in what goes on in the community, who give of themselves when help is needed, and who may take leadership roles in activities not specifically connected to the church.

The role is far too important for a parish simply to accept any volunteers who present themselves. Sometimes individuals come forward who want to minister out of their own needs or who may have an inaccurate sense of what their own gifts are— or what gifts they lack. Such persons can destroy a community rather than build it up. The call to minister is more likely authentic when a community invites to serve it people who appear to have the necessary gifts and leadership qualities.

Formation: An Absolute Necessity

It is unfair both for those called on to lead the community's prayer and for the community itself to expect these leaders to preside without training and formation. As a starting point, basic formation of leaders takes place when all liturgy in the parish is celebrated with adequate preparation and care. Many dioceses conduct programs for lay ministers' formation, programs which usually include scripture, prayer, the church, and ministry among their topics. Such formation is recommended, if not imperative.

Above all, the leaders need training in understanding what liturgy and the church's liturgical tradition are, how the church prays, and what liturgical principles will help the community to worship as church. These leaders will require workshop sessions that develop the personal skills they need and help them become familiar with the structure and the various elements in each part of the celebration. They will want to meet with the other ministers involved, including those who lead the music, keeping in mind that no one leads in isolation. Everything is done for and with the community. Before a leader presides for the first time, a "walk-through" session is a must so that participants can look after all the details: where to place the book, the place from which he or she will lead each part of the ritual, and so on. Not only will this give the leader the confidence to lead in a prayerful manner, but it will also allow him or her to become transparent for the Spirit's work in the community.

Public Recognition

When leaders have received the formation and training that is expected, a public blessing is in order, if not by the bishop of the diocese, then by the pastor of the parish where they will serve. Not only will this blessing add a certain "official" character to the ministry, but it will also give an opportunity for members of the parish to pray for them and voice the parish's support. A bishop in Tanzania asks not only the priests in his diocese but also all the leaders of Sunday non-eucharistic liturgies to gather for the celebration of the Chrism Mass; these prayer leaders are also blessed and mandated for the ministry they perform. It gives them more authority when they lead their community's prayer, this bishop explained.

Some dioceses ask leaders for a commitment of a given period of time, such as three years, at which point these people may commit themselves to another period or step aside for others to replace them. Although a parish technically needs only one person to lead Sunday worship, it is important that communities which need lay leaders of prayer make sure that several people, even several teams, are prepared for this ministry. These teams often divide tasks among themselves, not just to avoid the perception that any one person is a little "holier," but also for mutual support. The *Sunday Celebration of the Word and Hours* (p.256) suggests that a communion minister may preside at the communion service; often one person will preside and another will give the homily or reflection. When several persons are involved, take care to maintain a sense of unity in the liturgy. Too much shifting back and forth from one person to another can be disconcerting.

Once lay persons begin their ministry of leading the community's prayer, they will want to continue training and formation both for their own growth in faith and deepening of their

Christian living, and to help them grow in their understanding of their role as leaders of prayer. As well, they will have an opportunity to evaluate what they are doing and to refine their skills. Meeting with others involved in the same ministry will also foster mutual support, providing an opportunity to build a community among lay presiders, not only within a parish but with those from neighbouring parishes.

In Summary

1. The presider's role is to lead the members of the body of Christ in their prayer. The liturgy, therefore, belongs to the whole community, not to the presider.

2. Organizational skills and the ability to communicate help the presider to allow the presence of God to shine through in the community's worship.

3. Formation and training are necessary for individuals called forth by a parish for this important ministry.

Discussion Questions

1. What is the presider's relationship to the assembly? Using the description in this chapter, reflect on your experience of various presiders, both ordained and lay. What experiences have been most helpful to your expression of faith? Why?

2. Too often lay presiders mirror poor presiding skills that they have absorbed from watching presbyters preside. What, in your opinion, are the skills that presiders, both lay and ordained, need to develop?

CHAPTER 4

The Focus of Non-eucharistic Sunday Worship

Vatican II's *Constitution on the Sacred Liturgy* tells us that, when the scriptures are proclaimed in the liturgy, God speaks to us, and that, in the gospel, Christ speaks to us here and now. Besides being present in the assembly, Christ is present in the proclamation of the Word (*CSL*, #7). When God speaks, God acts; therefore when the word of God is spoken in the community God is acting in that community, offering his saving gift at that moment. We tell, not just the story of what God has done in the past, but also the story of what God is doing for us right now.

Proclamation: An Act of Worship

Reading God's word aloud in the liturgy is an act of worship. God speaks to this assembly, at this time, in this place, and God's message will never be spoken in the same way again. It is an expression of God's relationship to this particular group of people.

When a community gathers for Sunday worship but is unable to celebrate the eucharist because no bishop or priest is present, the community celebrates God's word, hearing God speak to them and responding with prayer and thanksgiving, although the fullest expression of thanksgiving, the eucharist, is not possible at that time.

The liturgy of the word, then, is the core, the essence, of a community's non-eucharistic Sunday celebration. This liturgy unfolds in almost the same manner as that in any Sunday eucharist and is prepared with the same care. The role of the ministers, the lectors and the psalm cantor is based on the same principles.

Ongoing Formation in the Scriptures

Those who preside at this liturgy will also want to be inspired by God's word in order to lead the assembly in proclaiming, listening to and responding to that word. The kind of training that is provided to lectors by a parish or diocese is a prerequisite for the leaders. Not only do leaders also need skills for public reading, but they also need to understand that the heart of their ministry is the proclamation of God's word, which makes God present in this community. This understanding will help them better make that word of God come alive for their community. Above all, the leaders will want to give time on a regular, even daily, basis to read and reflect on the scriptures and to use every opportunity to learn what they have to say to us.

Certainly those who are called on to share a reflection will want to avail themselves of every opportunity to deepen their knowledge and understanding of the scriptures. The function of this shared reflection or homily is to connect the word of God to the lives of those in that particular community. It is not an opportunity for instruction, since the liturgy is first of all celebration, although well-prepared and good celebration of the liturgy is the best teacher of faith that we have.

It has been said that those who preach should have the Bible in one hand and the newspaper in the other. Particularly here, knowing God's ways in the community and knowing the community's struggles, difficulties and strengths, make it easier for the leader to truly break open God's Word. Many who are called on to present a shared reflection find it very helpful to gather with others in the community to reflect on the scriptures of the Sunday, share their insights, and build their own reflection from what they have heard.

In Summary

1. God is present whenever the scriptures are proclaimed in worship.

2. The liturgy of the word is the essence of non-eucharistic Sunday worship.

3. Presiders need to steep themselves in the scriptures and to have the same skills to proclaim God's word as lectors.

Discussion Questions

1. What is the significance of the liturgy of the word in a non-eucharistic Sunday liturgy?

2. What opportunities for ongoing formation in scripture exist in your diocese or region? Which would be appropriate for lay presiders?

CHAPTER 5

Liturgical Principles for Lay Leaders

Does a Sunday celebration of God's word without eucharist deserve the same attention as the eucharist itself? Yes, it does. Since all of the church's liturgy is a celebration of the paschal mystery, the church must have the same concern about the liturgy celebrated when the eucharist is not possible as it does for the eucharist itself. Knowing the principles of good liturgical celebration liturgy is certainly helpful.

Ritual Creates the Encounter with God

1. Keep in mind that liturgy is first of all ritual, the ritual that makes the community's encounter with God in its prayer possible. As ritual, the liturgy belongs to the community, to the church. Its elements that are repeated and, thus, familiar, allow the community to enter fully into worship. These elements are not changed unless there is a very good reason for doing so. Good ritual needs no explanation; it has many valid layers of meaning, and will mean something different to different people at different times.

Be Authentic

2. Be yourself in the presence of God, that is, be human. Be authentic, not phoney, and do not adopt a "pulpit voice" or an "obviously religious," affected style.

3. Be so well prepared that you truly own what you do and say; only then can you serve the assembly. When the prayer is your prayer, the community can more easily make it their

prayer. Fear and nervousness will not get in the way and call attention to yourself.

Every Little Thing Counts

4. Everything you do—walking, bowing, gestures, sitting, etc.—expresses the prayer of the community. Whatever you do gives a signal that either supports the prayer of the community or hinders it.

5. Being a leader of prayer means being a model of prayer; a presider participates in all of the community's prayer: singing, listening, reflective silence, spoken responses. Do this without dominating, fully aware of what your own gifts are, and with respect for the leadership of those in other roles.

Do One Thing At A Time

6. In good ritual action only one thing happens at a time and there is only one focal point at a time. Ministers cannot walk and bow at the same time, or listen attentively if they are pre-occupied with what is coming, or turning pages to find the next text. Those responsible must prepare every element of the rite ahead of time so that, as leaders, they can be totally present to the liturgy at that moment. Focus, for example, on the reader who is proclaiming the word; sing the psalm response.

Reverence

7. Reverence is an essential quality of prayerful liturgy. A cele-bration of the liturgy that gives a sense of reverence is unhur-ried and deliberate; the words are said or sung with care; even simple actions such as walking from one place to another are carried out carefully. "Reverence has everything to do with the right pace, the right timing. When liturgy is the work of the whole person, the spirit with the body, then the beauty of praying makes for this reverent pace. The litur-gical way of doing something is not efficient; hurrying liturgy

can only make it seem foolish" (Gabe Huck, *Liturgy with Style and Grace*, revised ed., p. 37).

Reverence in the liturgy is also evident in how the ministers handle liturgical objects, such as books, vessels, candles, the cross. Hold these up in both hands as you would carry any precious object. When using ritual gestures, such as extending your arms in a gesture of welcome during the opening greeting, perform each gesture deliberately and with full and bold expression. If a leader chooses to use the *orans* gesture (the posture with the forearms directed upwards from the elbow, indicating that our prayer is directed to God, and the hands open, indicating that the whole world is included) for the opening prayer, it is done with both hands and, again, in a deliberate manner. Performing these gestures with one hand while holding a book in the other belittles the gesture. If you must hold the book, do not use these gestures.

The role of silence

Silence is a necessary ingredient to celebrating with reverence. Silence is not optional; it must be taken seriously. Not only does observing silence at the places called for prevent us from rushing the liturgy, but it also allows the words or actions to reach more deeply into our minds and hearts.

The Whole Body at Worship

8. Use your whole body to give the message that what you are doing is important. Eye contact is essential; after all, it is the community's prayer you are leading, not your own, and looking at those assembled is both respectful and hospitable. Very ordinary human body language can convey your reverence for the presence of Christ in this community and your reverence for the prayer of this community.

Necessary Formality

9. Being hospitable does not mean being familiar and casual. Because liturgy is ritual action, there is a certain level of formality needed to give it dignity, but that dignity does not mean the presider is aloof, cold, unfeeling. Warmth and sincerity can be more appropriately conveyed through one's manner, facial expression and tone of voice than through a chatty flow of words. Liturgy is intended to celebrate the good news of God's gifts, creation and redemption, and is therefore a joyous occasion. But the liturgy is not entertainment, and the presider's role is not that of an entertainer. A talk-show-host kind of style is not appropriate.

In Summary

1. Observing liturgical principles will help presiders lead the community in prayerful worship.

2. A sense of reverence can more easily be projected by an unhurried and deliberate manner and observing appropriate times of silence.

3. To celebrate the liturgy, you will need to balance warmth and hospitality with dignity and formality.

Discussion Question

1. Examine each of the principles outlined in this chapter. Which do you find most surprising? Which would be most difficult to implement or enhance in your situation? Why?

CHAPTER 6

The Shape
of a Sunday
Celebration
of the Word

Before looking at the structure of the ritual, those who lead it might remind themselves that the liturgy, as the public prayer of those called together by God to worship and give thanks, is something larger than ourselves or the local community; we have received it from the church. Knowing the tradition and the structure of liturgical prayer in the Roman Rite is at least very helpful, if not necessary, to understand the ritual. This knowledge will help avoid the "do-your-own-thing" kind of approach to preparing this liturgy.

No Second-rate Liturgy

A Sunday celebration of the word is not second-rate liturgy; it is the ritual prayer of the people of God, of Christ and the members of his body, and should be prepared with the same care as any celebration of the eucharist. Hospitality is also just as important; out of reverence for the presence of Christ in this gathering we welcome each other and welcome the stranger.

The new ritual book recently published by the Canadian bishops for the church in Canada, *Sunday Celebration of the Word and Hours*, has all the spoken texts required by anyone leading this liturgy, including the opening prayers throughout the liturgical year. As well, extensive liturgical notes and "rubrics" (instructions printed in red that are not to be read aloud) are included throughout the book.

The Shape of the Liturgy

A general flow marks the shape of the church's public prayer. God calls his people and speaks to them through the word; the church responds in prayer and thanksgiving, and the people are dismissed to go and live what they just celebrated, nourished by God's word and the faith of the community.

In a Sunday celebration of the word, this shape is apparent in the four-part structure. First come the introductory rite, and the liturgy of the word, which concludes with a profession of faith and the general intercessions. Then follow a proclamation of praise (often followed by a communion rite), and a concluding rite.

The Introductory Rite

The introductory rite gathers the community who have answered God's call to assemble for worship as church, and draws those present into a united community that can pray with one voice. The first prayer of that community is the opening or gathering song; it is the community's "first act of worship." This song, be it a song of praise or a seasonal hymn, lets the assembly enter into this ritual, which is not just a human action, but Christ's action. Those preparing the music will want to select a song which is truly a song of praise in which the assembly can participate. One pastor has said that he can preach better when the assembly sings the opening song with enthusiasm and energy.

There is not, however, the usual entrance procession as in a eucharistic celebration. Instead of the ministers entering in procession during the opening song, the presider simply takes his or her place when the liturgy begins. A procession comes later, at the beginning of the liturgy of the word.

Following the opening song, the presider leads the community in the sign of the cross, a reminder of baptism, and greets the assembly with a liturgical greeting, that is, with a scriptural text. The community's response is a blessing of God. The presider then reminds the community that, although it cannot celebrate the eucharist, it still worships in union with the church and unites itself with neighbouring parishes.

Also part of the introductory rite is an opening or preparatory rite, which has a number of options including a penitential rite. Leaders might want to keep in mind that the introductory rites are meant to prepare the assembly to hear God's word rather than focus on reconciliation. We are reconciled by hearing God's word and being open to its message; the liturgy allows us to be reconciled *by* God's word, not reconciled *for* it.

The introductory rite ends with the opening prayer, the most important element in the rite. The ancient word for this prayer, the "collect," names what the prayer does: it collects the prayer in the hearts of all those present; the presider, following a period of silence during which the assembly brings its prayer to mind, voices that prayer. This prayer is not only universal, including all, but is also that proper to that Sunday. It belongs to the whole church and expresses the liturgical season.

The Liturgy of the Word

The procession just before the first reading highlights the essence of this liturgy, the celebration of God's word. This procession includes a reader who carries the lectionary, accompanied by two candle bearers. With the exception of this procession, the liturgy of the word is celebrated in the same manner as it is during a celebration of the eucharist. The readers prepare just as carefully and the gospel is proclaimed with ceremony to signify that Christ himself is speaking to the community. The psalm is sung, as is the gospel acclamation.

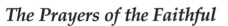

The Prayers of the Faithful

The general intercessions are the community's prayer for the needs of the whole world, the prayer in which the baptized exercise their priesthood by interceding for the world. The term, general, indicates just that—that the needs of the whole world are the material for the petitions that the community offers, through Christ, to the Father. If a lay presider is expected to prepare these petitions, he or she will want to be aware of the four areas suggested in the pastoral notes in the ritual. The petitions are statements expressing need, not exclamations of thanksgiving—a prayer of praise follows almost immediately. Nor are the petitions mini-homilies or bulletin boards.

Of course, these prayers reflect the community's own needs that surface when neighbours are concerned for each other. These intercessions, also called the prayers of the faithful because they are the prayers of the baptized, can help shape the personal prayer of members of the community. They remind the faithful to pray for these needs in their private prayer when, Sunday after Sunday, they hear the needs of the whole church and the world presented as well as the local community's needs.

Thanksgiving

A community's response to the word of God proclaimed in its midst includes intercession for God's reconciliation and healing in the world and thanksgiving for God's mighty works, especially for creation and for redemption. The Christian community expresses this thanksgiving most fully in celebrating eucharist.

Even when a community cannot celebrate the eucharist, it still praises God in other formulas, drawn from the psalms, from Paul's letters, from the prophet Daniel and from compositions of praise in the early church such as the *Te Deum*, or songs of praise. When the leader proclaims these texts of praise, the community responds by singing acclamations of praise.

These prayers of praise never include any texts from the eucharistic thanksgiving or its acclamations, the Sanctus, the memorial acclamation and the Great Amen. Nor do they include any of the actions of the eucharistic prayer, the preparation and presentation of the gifts, the offering of the gifts, or the breaking of bread.

The Communion Rite

Most communities then proceed to the communion rite, which begins with the greeting of peace and the Lord's Prayer, the pre-eminent prayer of all Christians. Bringing the reserved sacrament to the altar is done simply, in silence, reminding the community that the rite is not an entity in itself but part of the whole eucharistic action. The rite proceeds in a familiar manner, with a procession and a processional communion song, followed by silence and a concluding prayer. Catholics will want to continually remind themselves that sharing the eucharistic bread in this rite is participation in a celebration of the eucharist at another time and perhaps in a different place.

Concluding the Celebration

Following the prayer at the end of the communion rite and before the concluding rite, the community turns its attention to the affairs of the community by briefly making announcements and by taking up the collection to look after the needs of the pastor, parish and the poor.

Finally, the assembly is blessed, and dismissed to continue to respond to God's word by living the gospel in the world.

In Summary

1. A Sunday celebration of the word follows the general pattern of all liturgy: God calls and speaks to the community, and the people respond with praise and their lives of faith.

2. The prayer of praise is not a eucharistic prayer, and avoids the elements that belong to the eucharistic prayer.

3. The communion rite is to be seen as a part of a eucharist celebrated at another time and possibly in another place.

Discussion Questions

1. Evaluate your Sunday celebration of the word. Do you have the sense that God is speaking to you?

2. Is your celebration of the word filled with praise? How might the sense of praise be strengthened?

Preparing a Parish for Non-eucharistic Worship

When a parish community first comes face-to-face with the reality that the eucharist cannot be celebrated because a priest is no longer available, people can react with feelings of betrayal or abandonment. This is especially true when parishes which have always been served by a priest take for granted that one will always be available. Sometimes the illness or death of a pastor, and unavailability of a replacement deprive parishes of the eucharist without warning

All parishes which foresee a real possibility that a time will come when the community can no longer celebrate the eucharist every Sunday, as well as parishes that can no longer celebrate eucharist daily, should take steps to prepare themselves. This is the time for those responsible for the pastoral ministry of the parish to provide some catechesis on several aspects of the liturgical life of the church.

Catechesis

Many Catholics are unaware of the church's tradition of the liturgy of the hours. When daily eucharist is no longer possible, you can introduce the parish to morning and evening prayer, if these are not already being celebrated. Preparation would include instruction for the whole parish on the meaning and content of this form of prayer; the ritual itself would be carefully prepared and celebrated with the full participation of all those present.

Parish communities faced with not being able to celebrate the eucharist on Sunday will need reminders about the meaning of Sunday as the Day of the Lord. Point out that God still calls the community to gather as a community to worship, thus making the church visible. Parishioners will need to hear that the eucharist is the fullest expression of the church made visible, and that their desire for the eucharist is entirely justified. Yet God calls the community, even when it cannot celebrate eucharist.

Catechesis on the Meaning and Structure of the Eucharist

This new parish situation can also provide an opportunity for catechesis on the meaning and structure of the eucharist. This catechesis can lead parishioners to understand more clearly Christ's presence in the community and in the proclamation of the scriptures during worship. Such catechesis must emphasize the difference between the celebration of the eucharist and non-eucharistic worship. It must also point out that a variety of liturgical ministries are equally important to both celebrations, since both are the worship of the whole church.

Involve Parishioners in Discernment

As much as possible, parishioners should be involved in discerning who should be called on to lead the community's worship. They should be aware of the need for formation and training required for this role, and they may need to be reminded that these people need their prayer and support. Invite parishioners, especially as members of the assembly, to reflect on their own role in the liturgy.

Mutual Support

Sometimes knowing that other parishes are in the same situation gives parish communities support. It is helpful to be aware of the diocesan programs being offered and to know the local bishop's expectations.

New Responsibility

Parishes that continue to gather every Sunday, even if they cannot celebrate the eucharist, sometimes find that they have to take responsibility for their liturgy in a different way than when the priest presided. The full and active participation in the liturgy called for by Vatican II is sometimes more of a reality in non-eucharistic worship because people cannot simply "let the priest do it." At the same time, members of the parish often take more ownership of the whole life of the parish. When they are also concerned that the sick and dying receive pastoral care, and will look after them, the dismissal at Sunday worship has been heard as a call to serve.

In Summary

1. When a parish community can no longer celebrate the eucharist as it once did, the community will want to continue to respond to God's call to gather for worship.

2. The community seeks out those among them who have the gifts to lead them in prayer; it must provide for their formation and training.

3. The various liturgical ministries are also important in non-eucharistic worship.

Discussion Questions

1. When a parish is faced with the reality of no longer having a priest come to celebrate Sunday eucharist with it, what is the first step the parish can take?

2. Why is training for leaders important?

3. What resources does your diocese provide for parishes who cannot celebrate the eucharist every Sunday?

GLOSSARY

Assembly: the term used to describe the people who have gathered to worship together. The assembly as a whole celebrates the liturgy, and the presider is a member of the assembly.

Berakah: a Hebrew prayer form that usually begins by blessing God. Used by the Hebrews as a grace after meals, it is considered to be the basis of Christian eucharistic prayer.

Deacon: an ordained minister whose liturgical ministry includes preaching and presiding at baptisms and weddings. Some men are deacons for only a short time before they are ordained to the priesthood (transitional deacons); others are permanent deacons.

Liturgy: the name given to the official public prayer of the church of the Roman rite, including the celebration of all the sacraments, the liturgy of the hours and some other nonsacramental prayers such as funeral vigils. The word is derived from a Greek word meaning "work of the people."

Paschal mystery: the mystery of the life, death and resurrection of Christ that is always central to the church's celebration of the liturgy.

Proclamation: texts spoken, not primarily to give information, but to express faith and deep conviction.

Ritual: the actions and words of a community at prayer that, through repetition and a predictable pattern permit the community to encounter God and experience salvation.

Ritualism: going through the motions of a ritual without interiorizing the meaning of the rite.

Roman rite: the liturgical rites used by the bishop of Rome and other communities using the same tradition. It is one of at least seventeen major rites in the world.

Rubrics: from the Latin word for red. The name given to those texts printed in red in liturgical books. These texts are intended for instruction. They are not to be spoken.

Te Deum: a hymn of praise that begins, "You are God." It is used during the liturgy of the hours on Sundays when the Glory to God is used at the eucharist.

BIBLIOGRAPHY

Recommended Reading
Ritual books

Sunday Celebration of the Word and Hours, Ottawa, Canadian Catholic Conference of Bishops, Concacan, Inc., 1995. This ritual book, approved by the National Liturgy Office for use in Canada, comes in the large, hard-cover edition intended for use in the liturgy and a smaller soft-cover edition intended for preparation of the liturgy.

Sunday Celebrations in the Absence of a Priest: Leader's Edition. Collegeville, MN: The Liturgical Press, 1997. This ritual, approved for use in the United States by the United States National Conference of Bishops, is for use of deacons and lay persons who will lead such celebrations.

Books

Dallen, James. *The Dilemma of Priestless Sundays.* Foreword by Bishop William E. McManus. Chicago, Liturgy Training Publications, 1994. Explores the theological issues involved in Sunday non-eucharistic worship that includes a communion service.

Glendinning, Barry. *Preparing to Preside* and *Preparing to Preach.* Ottawa: Novalis, 1997. These two books in the *Preparing for Liturgy* series offer the fundamentals in these two important areas.

Henderson, J. Frank. *Preparing to Preach* and *Preparing to Preside.* Ottawa: Novalis, 1991. These two pamphlets deal with the most basic attitudes and skills needed for leading the community's prayer. Good introductory material.

Huck, Gabe. *Liturgy with Style and Grace*, revised edition. Chicago, Liturgy Training Publications, 1984. This book deals with the basics of the church's worship in general and treats many aspects of that worship, including the liturgical year. Its format, a two-page discussion on a given topic followed by reflection questions, makes for easy reading.

Hughes, Kathleen, RSCJ. *Lay Presiding: The Art of Leading Prayer.* Collegeville, MN, The Liturgical Press, 1988. This little book explores some aspects of the ministry of leading community prayer that one might not think of, such as the "discipline of creativity."

Articles

The Art of Presiding, *National Bulletin on Liturgy*, No. 134 (Vol. 27, Fall 1993). Included in this issue is a document published by the Association of National Liturgical Secretaries of Europe entitled *Leading the Prayer of God's People. Liturgical Presiding for Priests and Laity.* The document examines many of the issues of leading community prayer and offers some general principles. Well worth reading.

Pastoral Notes: Sunday Celebration of the Word and Hours, *Canadian Studies in Liturgy*, No. 6. National Liturgical Office. Canadian Conference of Catholic Bishops, Ottawa, 1995. This volume contains two important documents that deal with Sunday non-eucharistic Sunday worship, the 1988 document from the Congregation for Divine Worship entitled Directory for Sunday Celebrations in the Absence of a Priest and 1992 pastoral letter from the Canadian bishops entitled Sunday Celebrations of the Word: Gathering in the Expectation of the Eucharist. As well there is a section on the formation of leaders of prayer, material that is found only in this publication, and the liturgical notes also found in the ritual book itself but here gathered together.

Sunday Celebrations of the Word, *National Bulletin on Liturgy,* No. 139 (Vol. 27, Winter 1994). Ed. by J. Frank Henderson. Ottawa: Canadian Conference of Catholic Bishops.

Sunday Liturgy: When Lay People Preside. *National Bulletin on Liturgy*, No. 79 (Vol. 14, May-June 1981). This issue offers some reflections on the meaning of the Lord's Day and on the structure of such a Sunday liturgy.

Videos

Brooks-Leonard, John, Hughes, RSCJ, Kathleen, and Bernstein, CSJ, Eleanor. *Leading the Community in Prayer: The Art of Presiding for Deacons and Lay Persons.* Collegeville, MN, The Liturgical Press, 1989. A 76-minute video. Through discussion and demonstration, viewers learn the significance of the actions and words that constitute the ministry of public prayer.

Malloy, Patrick. *Lay-Led Sunday Worship: Understanding "Sunday Celebrations in the Absence of a Priest".* Collegeville, MN: The Liturgical Press, 1996. A 30-minute video. Lay-Led Sunday Worship focuses on the experience of three parishes in Montana and also a seminar held for lay leaders of prayer at St. John's University, Collegeville, Minnesota. The video explains the structure of the service in Sunday Celebrations in the Absence of a Priest and the reactions of parishioners, presiders and priests to this form of Catholic Sunday liturgy.

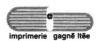

imprimerie gagné ltée